Copyright ©2017 by Gerald .O

ISBN- 13: 978-1981286607

DEDICATION

This book is dedicated first, to all lovers of Bitcoins;
Then to Wiki team, who made
this work possible .

Contents

- 14 21 million coins isn't enough; doesn't scale
- 15 Bitcoins are stored in wallet files, just copy the wallet file to get more coins!
- 16 Lost coins can't be replaced and this is bad
- 17 It's a giant ponzi scheme
- 18 Finite coins plus lost coins means deflationary spiral
- 19 Bitcoin can't work because there is no way to control inflation
- 20 The Bitcoin community consists of anarchist/conspiracy theorist/gold standard 'weenies'
- 21 Anyone with enough computing power can take over the network
- 22 Bitcoin violates governmental regulations
- 23 Fractional reserve banking is not possible
- 24 After 21 million coins are mined, no one will generate new blocks
- 25 Bitcoin has no built-in chargeback mechanism and this is bad
- 26 Quantum computers would break Bitcoin's security
- 27 Bitcoin makes self-sufficient artificial intelligence possible
- 28 Bitcoin mining is a waste of energy and harmful for ecology
- 29 Shopkeepers can't seriously set prices in bitcoins because of the volatile exchange rate

- 30 Like Flooz and e-gold, bitcoins serve as opportunities for criminals and will be shut down
- 31 Bitcoins will be shut down by the government just like Liberty Dollars were
- 32 Bitcoin is not decentralized because the developers can dictate the software's behavior
- 33 Bitcoin is a pyramid scheme
- 34 Bitcoin was hacked

Misconception one

Bitcoin is just like all other digital currencies; nothing new

Nearly all other digital currencies are centrally controlled. This means that:

- They can be printed at the subjective whims of the controllers
- They can be destroyed by attacking the central point of control
- Arbitrary rules can be imposed upon their users by the controllers

Being decentralized, Bitcoin solves all of these problems.

Misconception Two

Bitcoins don't solve any problems that fiat currency and/or gold doesn't solve

Unlike gold, bitcoins are:

- Easy to transfer
- Easy to secure
- Easy to verify

- Easy to granulate

Unlike fiat currencies, bitcoins are:

- Predictable and limited in supply
- Not controlled by a central authority (such as The United States Federal Reserve)
- Not debt-based

Unlike electronic fiat currency systems, bitcoins are:

- Potentially anonymous
- Freeze-proof
- Faster to transfer
- Cheaper to transfer

Misconception Three

Miners, developers or some other entity could change Bitcoin's properties to benefit themselves

Bitcoin's properties cannot be illegitimately changed as long as most of bitcoin's economy uses full node wallets. Transactions are irreversible and uncensorable as long as no single coalition of miners has more than 50% hash power and the transactions have an appropriate number of confirmations.

Bitcoin requires certain properties to be enforced for it to be a good form of money, for example:

1. Nobody ever created money out of nothing (except for miners, and only according to a well-defined schedule).
2. Nobody ever spent coins without knowing their private key.
3. Nobody spent the same coin twice
4. Nobody violated any of the other tricky rules that are needed to make the system work (difficulty, proof of work, DoS protection, ...).

These rules *define* bitcoin. A full node is software that verifies the rules of bitcoin. Any transaction which breaks these rules is not a valid bitcoin transaction and would be rejected in the same way that a careful goldsmith rejects fool's gold.

Full node wallets should be used by any intermediate bitcoin user or above and especially bitcoin businesses. Therefore anybody attempting to create bitcoins with invalid properties will find themselves being rejected by any trading partners. Note that lightweight wallets and web wallets do not have the low-trust benefits of full node wallets. Lightweight (SPV) wallets will blindly trust the miners, meaning if 51% of miners printed infinite coins or spent the same coin twice then lightweight wallet users would happily accept these fake bitcoins as payment. Web wallets blindly trust the web server which could display anything at all.

Miners are required to choose between multiple *valid* transaction histories. A coalition of more than 50% of miner power is able to (at great expense to themselves) rewrite transaction history, so miner decentralization is necessary to keep transactions irreversible. Miners burn a lot of electrical power in the mining process so they must constantly be trading their bitcoin income in order to pay bills. This makes miners utterly dependent on the bitcoin economy at large and therefore gives them a strong incentive to mine *valid* bitcoin blocks that full nodes will accept as payment.

Influential figures in the community (such as developers, politicians or investors) may try to use their influence to convince people to download and run modified full node software which changes bitcoin's properties in illegitimate ways. This is unlikely to succeed as long as counterarguments can freely spread through the media, internet forums and chatrooms. Many bitcoin users do not follow the bitcoin forums on a regular basis or even speak English. All appeals to run alternative software should be looked at critically for whether the individual agrees with the changes being proposed.

Full node software should always be open source so any programmer can examine the changes for themselves. Because of the co-ordination problem, there is usually a strong incentive to stick with the status quo.

Misconception Four

Bitcoin is backed by processing power

It is not correct to say that Bitcoin is "backed by" processing power. A currency being "backed" means that it is pegged to something else via a central party at a certain exchange rate yet you cannot exchange bitcoins for the computing power that was used to create them. Bitcoin is in this sense not backed by anything. It is a currency in its own right. Just as gold is not backed by anything, the same applies to Bitcoin.

The Bitcoin currency is *created* via processing power, and the integrity of the block chain is *protected* by the existence of a network of powerful computing nodes from certain attacks.

Misconception Five

Bitcoins are worthless because they aren't backed by anything

One could argue that gold isn't backed by anything either. Bitcoins have properties resulting from the system's design that allows them to be subjectively valued by individuals. This valuation is demonstrated when individuals freely exchange for or with bitcoins. Please refer to the Subjective Theory of Value.

Misconception Six

The value of bitcoins are based on how much electricity and computing power it takes to mine them

This statement is an attempt to apply to Bitcoin the labor theory of value, which is generally accepted as false. Just because something takes X resources to create does not mean that the resulting product will be worth X. It can be worth more, or less, depending on the utility thereof to its users.

In fact the causality is the reverse of that (this applies to the labor theory of value in general). The cost to mine bitcoins is based on how much they are worth. If bitcoins go up in value, more people will mine (because mining is profitable), thus difficulty will go up, thus the cost of mining will go up. The inverse happens if bitcoins go down in value. These effects balance out to cause mining to always cost an amount proportional to the value of bitcoins it produces

Misconception Seven

Bitcoin has no intrinsic value (unlike some other things)

This is simply not true. Each bitcoin gives the holder the ability to embed a large number of short in-transaction messages in a globally distributed and timestamped permanent data store, namely the bitcoin blockchain. There is no other similar datastore which is so widely distributed. There is a tradeoff between the exact number of messages and how quickly they can be embedded. But as of December 2013, it's fair to say that one bitcoin allows around 1000 such messages to be embedded, each within about 10 minutes of being sent, since a fee of 0.001 BTC is enough to get transactions confirmed quickly. This message embedding certainly has intrinsic value since it can be used to prove ownership of a document at a certain time, by including a one-way hash of that document in a transaction. Considering that electronic notarization services charge something like $10/document, this would give an intrinsic value of around $10,000 per bitcoin.

While some other tangible commodities do have intrinsic value, that value is generally much less than its trading price. Consider for example that gold, if it were not used as an inflation-proof store of value, but rather only for its industrial uses, would certainly not be worth what it is today, since the industrial requirements for gold are far smaller than the available supply thereof.

In any event, while historically intrinsic value, as well as other attributes like divisibility, fungibility, scarcity, durability, helped establish certain commodities as mediums of exchange, it is certainly not a prerequisite. While bitcoins are accused of lacking 'intrinsic value' in this sense, they make up for it in spades by possessing the other qualities necessary to make it a good medium of exchange, equal to or better than commodity money.

Another way to think about this is to consider the value of bitcoin the global network, rather than each bitcoin in isolation. The value of an individual telephone is derived from the network it is connected to. If there was no phone network, a telephone would be useless. Similarly the value of an individual bitcoin derives from the global network of bitcoin-enabled merchants, exchanges, wallets, etc... Just like a phone is necessary to transmit vocal information through the network, a bitcoin is necessary to transmit economic information through the network.

Value is ultimately determined by what people are willing to trade for - by supply and demand.

Misconception Eight

Bitcoin is illegal because it's not legal tender

In March 2013, the U.S. Financial Crimes Enforcement Network issues a new set of guidelines on "de-centralized virtual currency", clearly targeting Bitcoin. Under the new guidelines, "a user of virtual currency is not a Money Services Businesses (MSB) under FinCEN's regulations and therefore is not subject to MSB registration, reporting, and record keeping regulations." Miners, when mining bitcoins for their own personal use, aren't required to register as a MSB or Money Transmitter.

In general, there are a number of currencies in existence that are not official government-backed currencies. A currency is, after all, nothing more than a convenient unit of account. While national laws may vary from country to country, and you should certainly check the laws of your jurisdiction, in general trading in any commodity, including digital currency like Bitcoin, BerkShares, game currencies like WoW gold, or Linden dollars, is not illegal.

Misconception Nine

Bitcoin is a form of domestic terrorism because it only harms the economic stability of the USA and its currency

According to the definition of terrorism in the United States, you need to do violent activities to be considered a terrorist for legal purposes. Recent off-the-cuff remarks by politicians have no basis in law or fact.

Also, Bitcoin isn't domestic to the US or any other country. It's a worldwide community, as can be seen in Bitcoin nodes.

Misconception Ten

Bitcoin will only enable tax evaders which will lead to the eventual downfall of civilization

Cash transactions offer an increased level of anonymity, yet are still taxed successfully. It is up to you to follow the applicable tax laws in your home country, or face the consequences.

While it may be easy to transfer bitcoins pseudonymously, *spending* them on tangibles is just as hard as spending any other kind of money anonymously. Tax evaders are often caught because their lifestyle and assets are inconsistent with their reported income, and not necessarily because government is able to follow their money.

Finally, the Bitcoin blockchain is a permanent record of all transactions, meaning it can be mined for info at any time in the future making investigation, tracing of funds, etc much easier than with other forms of payment.

Misconception Eleven

Bitcoins can be printed/minted by anyone and are therefore worthless

Bitcoins are not printed/minted. Instead, Blocks are computed by miners and for their efforts they are awarded a specific amount of bitcoins and transaction fees paid by others..

Misconception Twelve

Bitcoins are worthless because they're based on unproven cryptography

SHA256 and ECDSA which are used in Bitcoin are well-known industry standard algorithms. SHA256 is endorsed and used by the US Government and is standardized (FIPS180-3 Secure Hash Standard). If you believe that these algorithms are untrustworthy then you should not trust Bitcoin, credit card transactions or any type of electronic bank transfer. Bitcoin has a sound basis in well understood cryptography.

Misconception Thirteen

Early adopters are unfairly rewarded

Early adopters are rewarded for taking the higher risk with their time and money. The capital invested in bitcoin at each stage of its life invigorated the community and helped the currency to reach subsequent milestones. Arguing that early adopters do not deserve to profit from this is akin to saying that early investors in a company, or people who buy stock at a company IPO (Initial Public Offering), are unfairly rewarded.

This argument also depends on bitcoin early adopters using bitcoins to store rather than transfer value. The daily trade on the exchanges (as of Jan 2012) indicates that smaller transactions are becoming the norm, indicating trade rather than investment. In more pragmatic terms, "fairness" is an arbitrary concept that is improbable to be agreed upon by a large population. Establishing "fairness" is no goal of Bitcoin, as this would be impossible.

Looking forwards, considering the amount of publicity bitcoin received as of April 2013, there can be no reasonable grounds for complaint for people who did not invest at that time, and then see the value (possibly) rising drastically higher.

By starting to mine or acquire bitcoins today, you too can become an early adopter.

Misconception Fourteen

21 million coins isn't enough; doesn't scale

One Bitcoin is divisible down to eight decimal places. There are really 2,099,999,997,690,000 (just over 2 quadrillion) maximum possible atomic units in the bitcoin system.

The value of "1 BTC" represents 100,000,000 of these. In other words, each bitcoin is divisible by up to 10^8.

As the value of the unit of 1 BTC grew too large to be useful for day to day transactions, people started dealing in smaller units, such as milli-bitcoins (mBTC) or micro-bitcoins (μBTC).

Misconception Fifteen

Bitcoins are stored in wallet files, just copy the wallet file to get more coins!

No, your wallet contains your secret keys, giving you the rights to spend your bitcoins. Think of it like having bank details stored in a file. If you give your bank details (or bitcoin wallet) to someone else, that doesn't double the amount of money in your account. You can spend your money or they can spend your money, but not both.

Misconception Sixteen

Lost coins can't be replaced and this is bad

Bitcoins are divisible to 0.00000001, so there being fewer bitcoins remaining is not a problem for the currency itself. If you lose your coins, indirectly all other coins are worth more due to the reduced supply. Consider it a donation to all other bitcoin users.

A related question is: Why don't we have a mechanism to replace lost coins? The answer is that it is impossible to distinguish between a 'lost' coin and one that is simply sitting unused in someone's wallet. And for amounts that are provably destroyed or lost, there is no census that this is a bad thing and something that should be re-circulated.

Misconception Seventeen

It's a giant ponzi scheme

In a Ponzi Scheme, the founders persuade investors that they'll profit. Bitcoin does not make such a guarantee. There is no central entity, just individuals building an economy.

A Ponzi scheme is a zero sum game. In a ponzi scheme, early adopters can only profit at the expense of late adopters, and the late adopters always lose. Bitcoin can have a win-win outcome. Earlier adopters profit from the rise in value as Bitcoin becomes better understood and in turn demanded by the public at large. All adopters benefit from the usefulness of a reliable and widely-accepted decentralized peer-to-peer currency.

It is also important to note that I Satoshi Nakamoto, the creator of bitcoin, has never spent a bitcoin (other than giving them away when they were worthless) which we can verify by checking the blockchain.

Misconception Eighteen

Finite coins plus lost coins means deflationary spiral

As deflationary forces may apply, economic factors such as hoarding are offset by human factors that may lessen the chances that a Deflationary spiral will occur.

Misconception Ninteen

Bitcoin can't work because there is no way to control inflation

Inflation is simply a rise of prices over time, which is generally the result of the devaluing of a currency. This is a function of supply and demand. Given the fact that the supply of bitcoins is fixed at a certain amount, unlike fiat money, the only way for inflation to get out of control is for demand to disappear. Temporary inflation is possible with a rapid adoption of Fractional Reserve Banking but will stabilize once a substantial number of the 21 million "hard" bitcoins are stored as reserves by banks.

Given the fact that Bitcoin is a distributed system of currency, if demand were to decrease to almost nothing, the currency would be doomed anyway.

The key point here is that Bitcoin as a currency can't be inflated by any single person or entity, like a government, as there's no way to increase supply past a certain amount.

Indeed, the most likely scenario, as Bitcoin becomes more popular and demand increases, is for the currency to increase in value, or deflate, until demand stabilizes.

Misconception Twenty

The Bitcoin community consists of anarchist/conspiracy theorist/gold standard 'weenies'

The members of the community vary in their ideological stances. While it may have been started by ideological enthusiasts, Bitcoin now speaks to a large number of regular pragmatic folk, who simply see its potential for reducing the costs and friction of global e-commerce.

Misconception Twenty One

Anyone with enough computing power can take over the network

That said, as the network grows, it becomes harder and harder for a single entity to do so. Already the Bitcoin network's computing power is quite ahead of the world's fastest supercomputers, together.

What an attacker can do once the network is taken over is quite limited. Under no circumstances could an attacker create counterfeit coins, fake transactions, or take anybody else's money. An attacker's capabilities are limited to taking back their own money that they very recently spent, and preventing other people's transactions from receiving confirmations. Such an attack would be very costly in resources, and for such meager benefits there is little rational economic incentive to do such a thing.

Furthermore, this attack scenario would only be feasible for as long as it was actively underway. As soon as the attack stopped, the network would resume normal operation.

Misconception Twenty Two

Bitcoin violates governmental regulations

There is no known governmental regulation which disallows the use of Bitcoin.

Misconception Twenty Three

Fractional reserve banking is not possible

It is possible. Fractional Reserve Banking with Bitcoin is possible and practical. It is already implemented with CoinLenders. There is no fundamental difference between classical currencies and Bitcoin as it applies to banking. Banks will still be free to take in bitcoins and present them to customers as "available for withdrawal" while still lending most of those bitcoins to a different customer for a profit. Some of those bitcoins will be held in reserves in case of a bank run. It will be up to the bank to hold a sufficient supply of reserves in order to prevent insolvency in the event of a bank run. Central banks were established to enforce reserve requirements and so, with Bitcoin lacking a central bank, some banks will almost surely collapse, taking their customers' deposits with them. A large bitcoin exchange could tomorrow lend out 10,000 bitcoins to an individual to start a business. The money supply would thus increase by 10,000 and we would instantly have Fractional Reserve Banking. The same amount of bitcoins would still exist in the Block Chain, but the body of people participating in the Bitcoin economy would have the perception that more bitcoins exist. If the value of a bitcoin is stable for a long period of time, then Fractional Reserve Banking is *inevitable* .

Misconception Twenty Four

After 21 million coins are mined, no one will generate new blocks

When operating costs can't be covered by the block creation bounty, which will happen some time before the total amount of BTC is reached, miners will earn some profit from transaction fees. However unlike the block reward, there is no coupling between transaction fees and the need for security, so there is less of a guarantee that the amount of mining being performed will be sufficient to maintain the network's security.

Misconception Twenty Five

Bitcoin has no built-in chargeback mechanism and this is bad

Bitcoin base-layer transactions are final and irreversible by design, but consumer protection can still built into bitcoin in other layers on top. The most practical way of doing this is multisig escrow. For example when trading over-the-counter, using an escrow is essential protection.

It's worth noting that virtually all successful consumer-facing bitcoin businesses do indeed already implement some kind of consumer protection; Routine escrow was used by Localbitcoins, Silk Road and the bitcoin ebay-site Bitmit. Others such as online bitcoin casinos rely on their long-standing reputation, while others such as Coinbase.com rely on the legal and regulatory system.

The bitcoin method of routinely using escrow has benefits over competitors like credit cards. The security of credit cards is not very good which results in higher costs overall and the possibility of payments being reversed for months afterwards. By contrast when bitcoins have been released to the seller from escrow, they cannot be reversed as the coins are truely in the seller's possession. The requirement to use real-life names for credit cards and PayPal also excludes unbanked people and those from countries with less developed financial infrastructure. There are also downsides like bitcoin is not yet as widely accepted as credit cards and is not a front for providing lines of credit.

Misconception Twenty Six

Quantum computers would break Bitcoin's security

While ECDSA is indeed not secure under quantum computing, quantum computers don't yet exist and probably won't for a while. The DWAVE system often written about in the press is, even if all their claims are true, not a quantum computer of a kind that could be used for cryptography. Bitcoin's security, when used properly with a new address on each transaction, depends on more than just ECDSA: Cryptographic hashes are much stronger than ECDSA under QC.

Bitcoin's security was designed to be upgraded in a forward compatible way and could be upgraded if this were considered an imminent threat (cf. Aggarwal et al. 2017, "Quantum attacks on Bitcoin, and how to protect against them").

The *risk* of quantum computers is also there for financial institutions, like banks, because they heavily rely on cryptography when doing transactions.

Misconception Twenty Seven

Bitcoin makes self-sufficient artificial intelligence possible

A theorized autonomous agent which utilizes humans to build itself and issues autonomous payments for improvement work done, is not a conscious entity. Whatever AI is possible, is not going to be magically more possible simply because it could incentivize human behaviour with pseudonymous Bitcoin payments.

Misconception Twenty Eight

Bitcoin mining is a waste of energy and harmful for ecology

No more so than the wastefulness of mining gold out of the ground, melting it down and shaping it into bars, and then putting it back underground again. Not to mention the building of big fancy buildings, the waste of energy printing and minting all the various fiat currencies, the transportation thereof in armored cars by no less than two security guards for each who could probably be doing something more productive, etc.

As far as mediums of exchange go, Bitcoin is actually quite economical of resources, compared to others.

Economic Argument 1

Bitcoin mining is a highly competitive, dynamic, almost perfect, market. Mining rigs can be set up and dismantled almost anywhere in the world with relative ease. Thus, market forces are constantly pushing mining activity to *places* and *times* where the marginal price of electricity is low or zero. These electricity products are cheap for a reason. Often, it's because the electricity is difficult (and wasteful) to transport, difficult to store, or because there is low demand and high supply. Using electricity in this way is a lot less wasteful than simply plugging a mining rig into the mains indiscriminately.

For example, Iceland produces an excess of cheap electricity from renewable sources, but it has no way of exporting electricity because of its remote location. It is conceivable that at some point in future Bitcoin mining will only be profitable in places like Iceland, and unprofitable in places like central Europe, where electricity comes mostly from nuclear and fossil sources.

Market forces could even push mining into innovative solutions that have an effective electricity consumption of *zero*. Mining always produces heat equivalent to the energy consumed - for example, 1000 watts of mining equipment produces the same amount of heat as a 1000 watt heating element used in an electric space heater, hot tub, water heater, or similar appliance. Someone already in a willing position to incur the cost of electricity for its heat value alone could run mining equipment specially designed to mine bitcoins while capturing and utilizing the heat produced, without incurring any energy costs beyond what they already intended to spend on heating.

(Note that this is just an example; mining will not always produce heat equivalent to the energy consumed because some energy is inevitably released as electromagnetic radiation, among others.)

Economic Argument 2

When the environmental costs of mining are considered, they need to be weighed up against the benefits. If you question Bitcoin on the grounds that it consumes electricity, then you should also ask questions like this: Will Bitcoin promote economic growth by freeing up trade? Will this speed up the rate of technological innovation? Will this lead to faster development of green technologies? Will Bitcoin enable new, border crossing smart grid technologies? …

Dismissal of Bitcoin because of its costs, while ignoring its benefits, is a dishonest argument. In fact, any environmental argument of this type is dishonest, not just pertaining to Bitcoin. Along similar lines, it could be argued that wind turbines are bad for the environment because making the steel structure consumes energy.

Ratio of Capital Costs versus Electrical Costs

The BFL Jalapeno hashes at 5.5 Gh/s using 30W. That device consumes about $40 per year in electricity (using U.S. residential average of about $0.15 per kWh.) But the device costs over $300 including shipping. Thus, just about a quarter of all costs over a two-year useful life goes to electricity. This compares to GPUs where more than 90% of costs over a two-year life went to electricity. Even more efficient designs can be expected in the future.

Misconception Twenty Nine

Shopkeepers can't seriously set prices in bitcoins because of the volatile exchange rate

The assumption is that bitcoins must be sold immediately to cover operating expenses. If the shopkeeper's back-end expenses were transacted in bitcoins as well, then the exchange rate would be irrelevant. Larger adoption of Bitcoin would make prices sticky. Future volatility is expected to decrease, as the size and depth of the market grows.

In the meantime, many merchants simply regularly pull the latest market rates from the exchanges and automatically update the prices on their websites. Also you might be able to buy a put option in order to sell at a fixed rate for a given amount of time. This would protect you from drops in price and simplify your operations for that time period.

Misconception Thirty

Like Flooz and e-gold, bitcoins serve as opportunities for criminals and will be shut down

- Visa, MasterCard, PayPal, and cash all serve as opportunities for criminals as well, but society keeps them around due to their recognized net benefit.
- Hopefully Bitcoin will grow to the point where no single organization can disrupt the network, or would be better served by helping it.
- Terrorists fly aircraft into buildings, but the governments have not yet abolished consumer air travel. Obviously the public good outweighs the possible bad in their opinion.
- Criminal law differs between jurisdictions.

Misconception Thirty One

Bitcoins will be shut down by the government just like Liberty Dollars were

Liberty Dollars started as a commercial venture to establish an alternative US currency, including physical banknotes and coins, backed by precious metals. This, in and of itself, is not illegal. They were prosecuted under counterfeiting laws because the silver coins allegedly resembled US currency.

Bitcoins do not resemble the currency of the US or of any other nation in any way, shape, or form. The word "dollar" is not attached to them in any way. The "$" symbol is not used in any way.

Bitcoins have no representational similarity whatsoever to US dollars.

Of course, actually 'shutting down' Liberty Dollars was as easy as arresting the head of the company and seizing the offices and the precious metals used as backing. The decentralized Bitcoin, with no leader, no servers, no office, and no tangible asset backing, does not have the same vulnerability.

Misconception Thirty Two

Bitcoin is not decentralized because the developers can dictate the software's behavior

The Bitcoin protocol has now been widely accepted as the standard by the community of miners and users.

Though the developers of the original Bitcoin client still exert influence over the Bitcoin community, their power to arbitrarily modify the protocol is very limited. Since the release of Bitcoin v0.3, changes to the protocol have been minor and always in agreement with community consensus.

Protocol modifications, such as increasing the block award from 25 to 50 BTC, are not compatible with clients already running in the network. If the developers were to release a new client that the majority of miners perceives as corrupt, or in violation of the project's aims, that client would simply not catch on, and the few users who do try to use it would find that their transactions get rejected by the network.

There are also other Bitcoin clients made by other developers that adhere to the Bitcoin protocol. As more developers create alternative clients, less power will lie with the developers of the original Bitcoin client.

Misconception Thirty Three

Bitcoin is a pyramid scheme

Bitcoin is nearly opposite of a pyramid scheme in a mathematical sense. Because Bitcoins are algorithmically made scarce, no exponential benefit is derived from introducing new users to use of it. There is a quantitative benefit in having additional interest or demand, but this is in no way exponential.

Misconception Thirty Four

Bitcoin was hacked

In the history of Bitcoin, there has never been an attack on the block chain that resulted in stolen money from a confirmed output. Neither has there ever been a reported theft resulting directly from a vulnerability in the original Bitcoin client, or a vulnerability in the protocol. Bitcoin is secured by standard cryptographic functions. These functions have been peer reviewed by cryptography experts and are considered unlikely to be breakable in the foreseeable future.

It is safe to say that the currency itself has never been 'hacked'. However, several major *websites* using the currency have been hacked, often resulting in high profile Bitcoin heists. These heists are misreported in some media as hacks on Bitcoin itself. An analogy: Just because someone stole US dollars from a supermarket till, doesn't mean that the US dollar as a currency has been 'hacked'.

Most bitcoin thefts are the result of inadequate wallet security. In response to the wave of thefts in 2011 and 2012, the community has developed risk-mitigating measures such as wallet encryption, support for multiple signatures, offline wallets, paper wallets, and hardware wallets. As these measures gain adoption by merchants and users, the number of thefts drop.